W9-CBR-747

iPod Shuffle Fan Book
Life Is a Playlist

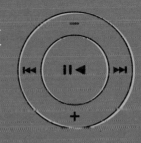

iPod Shuffle Fan Book
Life Is a Playlist

by J.D. Biersdorfer

Editor:	John Neidhart
Production Editor:	Darren Kelly
Creative Director:	Michele Wetherbee
Cover Designer:	Stefan Gutermuth *stefanart.com*
Interior Designer:	Anne Kilgore *paperwrk@twcny.rr.com*
Illustrators:	Robert Romano Jessamyn Read
Photographer:	Derrick Story
Copyeditor:	Nancy Reinhardt
Proofreader:	Philip Dangler
Indexer:	Johnna VanHoose Dinse

PRINT HISTORY

September 2005:   First Edition.

iPod
Shuffle
Fan Book

Contents

iPod
Shuffle
Fan Book

Contents

iPod
Shuffle
Fan Book

Getting Started with iPod Shuffle

Welcome to Planet iPod

"Life is random," say the advertisements for the iPod Shuffle, a battery-powered portable music player that can hold about 100 to 240 of your favorite songs and play them every which way and in any sequence the iPod Shuffle (or *you*) decide you want to hear them. There are literally a million possibilities to hear the same batch of songs played in an order you've never imagined.

If you've picked up *The iPod Shuffle Fan Book* to see what's inside, odds are you're thinking about getting an iPod Shuffle, have an iPod Shuffle (or another iPod model already), or maybe you just wanted to learn a little more about the world's littlest iPod without having to wade through a book five times the size of the Shuffle itself. Whatever the case, welcome aboard!

The iPod Shuffle is Apple Computer's lightest and least expensive iPod music player ever, and it works with both Windows and Macintosh computers. It has a lot in common with its older and bigger iPod siblings, but it also has a whole life of its own that's different from all other iPods, which is mostly what *The iPod Shuffle Fan Book* is about.

In this book, we'll go beyond the brief booklet that comes inside your Shuffle box and explain how to use an iPod Shuffle—everything from setting up your computer to connect the iPod Shuffle to loading up your favorite music so you can listen wherever you go. *The iPod Shuffle Fan Book* can also be thought of as *The iPod Shuffle Fun Book*, because we want to get you to the joy of iPodding as quickly as possible.

In addition to showing all the basics of Shuffle hardware and software to get you grooving fast, we'll also give you the details (and samples!) of one of the really great and creative features on any iPod ever made: making your own customized playlists of the songs *you* think should go together.

Yes, life is random, but learning how to use your iPod shouldn't be.

What makes an iPod Shuffle different?

All iPods were made to play music, but like cars, not all models look the same or can do all the same things.

The original iPod arrived in the hands of music lovers in 2001 and almost everyone knows what it looks like: a little white box the size of a deck of cards with a scroll wheel and an LCD screen you can use to find and play the songs stored on the iPod's hard drive. Even the smaller iPod Mini that came out a few years later still looked a bit like the original white iPod, except you could get it in different colors like pink and green.

When the iPod Shuffle went on sale in 2005, it was obviously a very different kind of iPod. It had no screen, no scroll wheel, and just a few simple buttons on the front and back. But the Shuffle was also much smaller than even the iPod Mini—tinier than a pack of bubble gum, and available in two memory sizes: 512 megabytes or 1 gigabyte of room to store songs. It was also light enough to wear around your neck so that you always had music within reach, even under your sweater at school or the office.

Getting
Started

iTunes

Filling Shuffle
with Music

Playing with
Playlists

Pocket USB
Drive

Cool Stuff for
iPod Shuffle

More Shuffle
Resources

iPod
Shuffle
Fan Book

4

Your songs will skip less if you bounce around with your iPod Shuffle, too. This is because the iPod Shuffle uses a solid chip of memory to store its songs and not a little hard drive with moving parts like the big iPods use.

But even though the iPod Shuffle is smaller all the way around, you still get to play plenty of music on it and you get to use the iPod's favorite program, iTunes, to load up your music player with music and audio books. So if you already have another iPod, you can use the same iTunes songs on your little iPod without having to buy or create new ones.

Even though it can't haul your entire collection around, the iPod Shuffle can still get you through a day of music. You can conveniently load up the Shuffle with songs from your existing (or future) iTunes library with the click of a button. And like its name says, you can quickly *shuffle*—play in a totally random order—the songs stored on your iPod Shuffle with the flick of a switch, or just play them in the order you originally loaded them.

Computer Requirements for iPod Shuffle

The iPod Shuffle has very specific system requirements for your computer. Make sure your Mac or PC meets them, or you'll have a lot of problems getting your iPod Shuffle to work at all.

Windows people need to have:

❶ Windows 2000 with Service Pack 4 (or later) or Windows XP (with Service Pack 2 or later).

❷ A PC with either a built-in USB port or third-party USB card installed.

❸ The iPod and iTunes software (included on the iPod Shuffle CD).

Macintosh owners need to have:

❶ Mac OS 10.2.8 or Mac OS 10.3.4 (or later).

❷ A Mac with a built-in USB port (not a third-party USB card).

❸ The iPod and iTunes software (included on the iPod Shuffle CD).

Getting
Started

iTunes

Filling Shuffle
with Music

Playing with
Playlists

Pocket USB
Drive

Cool Stuff for
iPod Shuffle

More Shuffle
Resources

iPod
Shuffle
Fan Book

6

The iPod CD

To make your computer and the iPod Shuffle talk to each other, you need to install the proper software onto your system, including the iTunes music program. The CD that comes with the iPod Shuffle has everything you need and it works for both Windows and Macintosh computers. You should install the software first before trying to use your iPod Shuffle.

The iPod CD has more than just software on it. You can find an electronic version of the User Guide and links to tutorials on the Web as well.

Installing the iPod software for Windows

To get started on your PC, insert the iPod CD into your computer's disc drive. On most systems, the CD will automatically start the installation process. Software wizards will walk you through the steps for installing the iPod Shuffle's software, iTunes, and the QuickTime multimedia programs on your PC.

If the CD does not automatically start installing the programs on your computer, choose My Computer→iPod CD→*iPodipodSetup.exe* to start it yourself.

After the installation process finishes, you should have a copy of iTunes 4.7.1 (or later) on your computer. If you had an older version of iTunes on there, all of your songs and playlists should show up in this new version.

The iPod CD also puts a copy of the iPod Updater software in your Programs menu. You don't need to run the iPod Updater now, but it's there in case you have problems with your iPod Shuffle and have to reinstall its software.

Installing the iPod software for Macintosh

You may already have a copy of iTunes on your Macintosh, especially because it comes free with all new iMacs, eMacs, PowerMacs, iBooks, and PowerBooks sold in the past few years. You need to make sure you have the *right* version of iTunes on your Mac, though.

You need iTunes 4.7.1 or later to use the iPod Shuffle. To see what version you have, choose iTunes→About iTunes on your Macintosh. If you don't have at least that version, install the new one from the CD that came with your iPod Shuffle.

Open the iTunes folder on the iPod CD and double-click the *iTunes4.mkpg* file. This installs the iPod Shuffle–happy version of iTunes on your Mac. You'll probably have to type in your Mac OS X administrator password to install the software.

After you have finished installing iTunes, open the iPod Installer folder on the iPod CD and double-click on the *iPod2005-01-11.pkg* file. (This file may have a slightly different name, depending on when you bought you Shuffle and when Apple last updated the iPod CD.)

Getting
Started

iTunes

Filling Shuffle
with Music

Playing with
Playlists

Pocket USB
Drive

Cool Stuff for
iPod Shuffle

More Shuffle
Resources

This action installs a copy of the iPod Updater program into your Mac's Applications→ Utilities→iPod Updater Software folder. While you don't necessarily need to run this in-staller file on the iPod Shuffle itself, having a copy of it stored on your Mac is helpful should you ever have technical woes severe enough that you have to reinstall the soft-ware for the Shuffle itself.

Plugging in the iPod Shuffle

After you have installed the software, you are ready to plug your iPod Shuffle into the computer.

Pull off the white plastic cap on the bottom of the Shuffle and plug its silver USB connec-tor into an available USB port on the computer. Make sure you plug the iPod Shuffle **all the way** into the port so the computer knows it's there.

If you have a computer like an iMac G3 or a PC where the USB ports are hard to get to or too close together for iPod Shuffle to plug in properly, you need to get an extension cable to plug into the computer's USB port that stretches far enough away so you have room to connect iPod Shuffle to the other end of the cable.

You can find a USB extension cable for less than $15 at most computer stores Or you can buy the iPod Shuffle Dock for about $30 from Apple or stores that sell iPod products.

The iPod Shuffle Dock plugs into your USB port and the little stand at the other end lets you plug in your Shuffle so it sits up at atten-tion for you.

Your new pal iTunes will open after a few seconds and ask you to name your Shuffle and register it with Apple. When you see the main iTunes window on your screen, your new iPod Shuffle will be listed in the iTunes Source pane, ready for you to add the music.

Getting
Started

iTunes

Filling Shuffle
with Music

Playing with
Playlists

Pocket USB
Drive

Cool Stuff for
iPod Shuffle

More Shuffle
Resources

All about USB and iPod Shuffle

Your iPod Shuffle connects to the USB port on your Macintosh or Windows computer. USB stands for Universal Serial Bus and it's been used to connect printers, scanners, keyboards, and other devices to computers since around 1997.

You use the computer's USB port to both charge up your iPod Shuffle's battery and load it up its memory with music.

There are two types of USB connections: USB 1.1 and USB 2.0. Both types of USB work for copying songs between computer and Shuffle, but USB 2.0 is much faster for transferring songs than USB 1.1, which is older and slower.

USB ports can carry power as well as data between your computer and another device, but not all USB ports have enough power to charge up the iPod Shuffle's battery. Most USB 2.0 ports and powered USB hubs have enough power, but some USB 1.1 ports or USB connectors on unpowered hubs or those found at the ends of Macintosh keyboards usually can't do it. If you have trouble powering your Shuffle from your USB ports, you may need to buy a powered hub.

iPod
Shuffle
Fan Book

Charging the iPod Shuffle's battery

The Shuffle has a rechargeable battery that you need to fill up with power after every 12 hours or so of iPod playtime.

After you connect the iPod Shuffle to the computer, the battery starts charging and a round amber light comes on, just above the control wheel. The amber light tells you the Shuffle is charging up. When the light turns green, the Shuffle is fully charged.

It takes about 2 hours to get the battery up to an 80 percent charge and 4 hours to fully charge the Shuffle battery. Make sure the computer doesn't slide into sleep mode while the Shuffle is charging, though, as this might interfere with the power transfer.

If you find your computer doesn't have USB ports that can charge up the Shuffle, you can get a USB power supply for $30 from the Apple Store that plugs into a wall outlet and provides a USB port for you to plug the iPod Shuffle right into.

Without a powered USB port, you can still plug your iPod Shuffle into the computer to update your songs, but you need to charge up its battery separately with the USB AC adapter.

Getting
Started

iTunes

Filling Shuffle
with Music

Playing with
Playlists

Pocket USB
Drive

Cool Stuff for
iPod Shuffle

More Shuffle
Resources

What the buttons do

The iPod Shuffle has a very simple set of buttons on the front and a sliding switch on the back, and these controls are all you need to operate the player.

Press the big round button in the middle of the iPod Shuffle's control ring to start playing a song. If you have a song playing, press the button again to pause it.

Press the plus (+) button to make the song louder or press the minus button (–) to lower the volume.

Press the >>| button to advance to the next song.

Press the |<< button on the other side of the ring to play the previous song again.

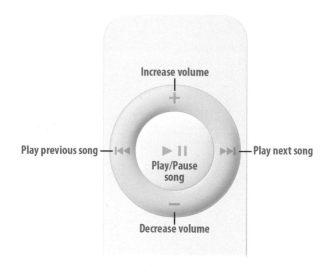

Increase volume

Play previous song ── Play/Pause song ── Play next song

Decrease volume

The sliding switch on the back of the iPod Shuffle controls how your songs are played. The switch can be kind of hard to move, but it works pretty well if you hold the Shuffle in one had and slide the switch with your thumb.

To turn the Shuffle off, slide the switch all the way to the top so that no green color is showing underneath.

To play all your songs in the order they are on your playlists, slide the switch down one notch to the middle icon that looks like two arrows chasing each other in a circle.

To mix up your songs and play them in a random order as the iPod Shuffle was designed to do for you, slide the switch all the way down to the bottom of the slot so that it's closest to the icon that looks like two arrows crossing over each other.

There's also a Battery Status light just below the switch that you can press to see how much of a charge is left in your iPod Shuffle's battery.

- **If you see a green light,** you have a good charge.
- **An amber light** means you need to charge up soon.
- **A red light** means your Shuffle is on the verge of running out of power.
- **No light** means you need to charge it up before you can use it again.

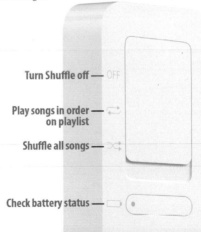

Turn Shuffle off ── OFF

Play songs in order on playlist ──

Shuffle all songs ──

Check battery status ──

Getting
Started

iTunes

Filling Shuffle
with Music

Playing with
Playlists

Pocket USB
Drive

Cool Stuff for
iPod Shuffle

More Shuffle
Resources

iPod
Shuffle
Fan Book

14

What the lights on the front mean

In addition to the Battery Status light on the back of the iPod Shuffle, the light that shines just above the control ring on the front of the player also tells you information about the iPod Shuffle's state of being.

A steady amber light means the Shuffle is in the process of charging its battery.

A blinking amber light means that you should not unplug the Shuffle from the computer because it's either updating new music onto its memory chip or working as a USB flash drive.

A steady green light, while plugged into the computer, means your Shuffle is fully charged.

This same green light will flash briefly when you tap the Play/Pause button to start a song and will blink for a minute when you press the button again to pause the music.

If you see *alternating green and amber lights* blinking at you when you press any of the control buttons, the Shuffle is acting up and probably needs to be reset; turn the switch on the back to the Off position for five seconds, and then slide it back to the Shuffle or Play In Order position.

The colored lights also tell you the *Hold status* of the iPod Shuffle. You can put the Shuffle into Hold mode by pressing down the center Play/Pause button for 3 seconds. The amber light blinks to indicate Hold is on. Press the same button again for 3 seconds to release the Shuffle from Hold. The green light blinks to indicate you have released your Hold.

If the iPod Shuffle is set to Hold and you press any of the buttons, the amber light flashes to tell you the Shuffle is in Hold mode.

Wearing and listening to the iPod Shuffle

The iPod Shuffle is not just a music player—it's a fashion statement that you can wear around your neck. Each iPod Shuffle comes with a plain plastic cap for when you want to carry it in your shirt or coat pocket, plus another white plastic cap attached to a lanyard for you to wear your Shuffle as a musical necklace while you walk or work.

To change caps, just pull the one you don't want off and snap the other one over the USB connector. When using the lanyard, make sure the iPod Shuffle is firmly attached so it doesn't fly off when you're wearing it around.

Just like all its other iPod relatives, the Shuffle also comes with its own set of white headphones with foam earbud covers. Plug these into the headphone jack on the top of the Shuffle.

You don't have to use these headphones, though, if you have a brand you like better or if you hate using earbud-style headphones because they hurt or always fall out of your ears. As long as they have the 3.5 mm stereo miniplug connecter, you can use any type of headphones designed for portable music players, including noise-canceling over-the-ear headphones or bass-enhanced earbuds.

Getting
Started

iTunes

Filling Shuffle
with Music

Playing with
Playlists

Pocket USB
Drive

Cool Stuff for
iPod Shuffle

More Shuffle
Resources

Taking care of the iPod Shuffle

As small as it is, the iPod Shuffle is still an electronic device and you should take care of it properly to keep it happy and working. Don't take it into the swimming pool with you or dip it in water to clean it because it is not waterproof!

If it does get dirty, make sure it's unplugged from the computer and wipe it gently with a damp, lint-free cloth. Do not spray it with household cleaner or polish.

Don't store your iPod Shuffle in extremely hot or cold places like a hot, parked car or in an unheated garage in the winter, because temperature can adversely affect it. Keep the iPod Shuffle in a safe place where the temperature is higher than –4 degrees and lower than 113 degrees Fahrenheit (or –20 degrees to 45 degrees Celsius).

Make sure the temperature is between 32 degrees and 95 degrees Fahrenheit (or 0 degrees and 39 degrees Celsius) wherever you are playing your iPod Shuffle.

Don't try to jam or force the USB connector into the computer's USB port when you plug in the Shuffle, It should snap in easily but firmly. If you have USB ports that are too close together, hard to reach, or set deep into the side of the computer, you'll need to get a USB extension cable to use with your Shuffle. Trying to shove it into the port may break both the USB port and your iPod Shuffle and then you'll be out of luck all the way around.

Keep the white plastic cap on the end of the iPod Shuffle when it's not connected to the computer so that the metal USB connector doesn't get bent or broken. Dirt or grime that gets into the USB connector can damage the inside and stop your Shuffle from making full contact with the computer.

Take care of your iPod Shuffle and it'll take care of you in moments of musical boredom!

iPod
Shuffle
Fan Book

iTunes: Can't Stop the Music

Getting Started

iTunes

Filling Shuffle
with Music

Playing with
Playlists

Pocket USB
Drive

Cool Stuff for
iPod Shuffle

More Shuffle
Resources

iPod
Shuffle
Fan Book

Digital music made easy with iTunes

Do you have a big stack of CDs full of music that you want to put on to your new iPod Shuffle but don't know how they get there? The answer, in one word, is *iTunes*.

Apple's iTunes program is a versatile jukebox for both Windows and Macintosh systems that converts your songs from CDs into iPod-friendly digital music files, lets you organize your vast library of songs and playlists, and even lets you rock out with music right at your computer. Even if you don't have your own CDs, there's another way to get music into iTunes—just download tracks from the iTunes Music Store, where there are more than a million songs to choose from.

This chapter will tell you how to use iTunes to *get* digital music files for the iPod Shuffle, and the next chapter tells you how to *transfer* them. If you already know how to rip songs in iTunes, just skip this chapter and go to the next one to see how the iPod Shuffle and iTunes get along.

The parts of the iTunes window

When you first open iTunes, you'll see a window full of different sections and controls.

These are the main areas of the full iTunes window:

Playback controls The familiar buttons to play, pause, fast-forward, and rewind the song on the screen, plus a volume slider.

Source list The Source list shows you all of your musical options available in iTunes, including files stored in the Library, Internet radio, playlists, CDs in the computer, and anything on your iPod Shuffle.

Status window The Status window shows the song currently playing and how much of it is left to hear.

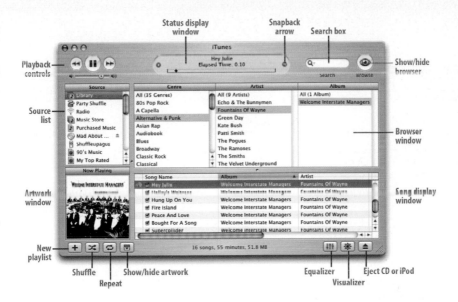

Status display window

Snapback arrow

Search box

Playback controls

Show/hide browser

Source list

Browser window

Artwork window

Song display window

New playlist

Shuffle

Repeat

Show/hide artwork

Equalizer

Visualizer

Eject CD or iPod

Browser The Browser shows you all of the songs you can listen to from your iTunes Library.

Search box If you think you have a song in your library but aren't sure, type its name here. You can also search for songs with certain words in the titles or for certain bands or singers.

Song display window You can see all of the songs from a select music source or playlist in the Song Display window.

Artwork window Songs you buy from the iTunes Music Store come with cover artwork, but you can also paste in your own photos for music you've ripped in iTunes.

Getting Started

iTunes

Filling Shuffle
with Music

Playing with
Playlists

Pocket USB
Drive

Cool Stuff for
iPod Shuffle

More Shuffle
Resources

Converting songs for iTunes

Right after you install the program, iTunes is ready to convert songs from your compact discs into digital music files that you can play on your iPod Shuffle. Converting an audio track from a CD is also called *ripping*.

This is what you do, in four easy steps. Ripping songs for the iPod works easiest if you are already connected to the Internet before you begin.

❶ Open iTunes and insert your compact disc into your computer's CD drive.

❷ Let iTunes use information on the CD to find and download the names of the songs, artist, and album from the Gracenote database of CDs on the Internet. (If iTunes doesn't download the information automatically, choose Advanced ›Get CD Track Names.)

❸ Make sure the names of all the songs you want to import into iTunes are checked. Uncheck the songs from the CD that you don't want to convert.

❹ Click the Import button in the top-right corner of the iTunes window.

Now you can sit back as iTunes converts the songs on your CD to digital music tracks. The program makes a green checkmark next to the name of every track converted, and shows an orange squiggle next to a track that's still in the process of converting.

When all the songs have been converted, you can eject the CD and play the song files in iTunes by double-clicking on the name of the song you want to hear or clicking on the title once to select it and then clicking the Play button at the top of the window.

Adding other digital music files to iTunes

If you have MP3 or other iTunes-friendly digital music files already on your computer, iTunes will offer to find and add them to its library the first time you start the program. If you don't add your assorted song files right then or want to add new ones later (that you haven't ripped directly in iTunes), you can easily add them to your collection.

Just choose File→Add to Library and locate the songs or folder of songs you want to add to your iTunes mix.

Options

You can see lots of information about the songs you have in iTunes, but you usually have to tell iTunes what you want to see.

To do this, choose File→View Options. A box comes up with all kinds of choices, including the year the album came out, the composer, the beats per minute of the song (helpful for making party playlists!), the date the song was added to iTunes, and many other bits of information about each and every song in the iTunes Library.

Just check the boxes for the items you want to see displayed in the iTunes window, and then click OK. You can adjust the size of any of the iTunes columns by clicking and dragging the edges of the columns around until you're satisfied.

Getting Started

iTunes

Filling Shuffle
with Music

Playing with
Playlists

Pocket USB
Drive

Cool Stuff for
iPod Shuffle

More Shuffle
Resources

Formats and bit rates

Not all digital music files are the same and even iTunes can't play every format out there. Because of its small size, the iPod Shuffle can play only *three* of the many formats available in iTunes, plus files that you buy and download from Audible.com and the iTunes Music Store. The Shuffle can't play files in the AIFF or Apple Lossless formats.

The formats that work with the iPod Shuffle are MP3, WAV, and AAC. By default, iTunes will encode your CD tracks into AAC files with a bit rate setting of 128 kilobits per second, which work perfectly on the iPod Shuffle. You can also encode your song files into the MP3 or WAV formats, which work on the iPod Shuffle and many other portable music players as well.

The *bit rate* of a song file has to do with sound quality and the amount of audio information encoded into it. Files with higher bit rate settings typically sound much better than files with lower bit rate settings, but the audio quality also varies with the encoding format you choose. The higher the bit rate, however, the more space a file tends to take up on your computer or iPod, because the additional audio data makes the file size larger.

The iTunes Music Store songs are also encoded as 128kbps AAC files. If you want the files you rip to sound better or take up less room, you can adjust the file-encoding settings in the iTunes Preferences box.

Changing the iTunes preferences

Want to make other adjustments with the way iTunes works? Choose iTunes→Preferences on the Mac or Edit→Preferences on your Windows version of iTunes. When you're ripping songs in iTunes, the main area of this box that you want to deal with is the Importing area. Click that icon or tab to go there.

In the Importing preferences, you can change the encoding format for your files from AAC to MP3 or WAV. Use the pop-up menu to change the bit rate for the files if you want, too.

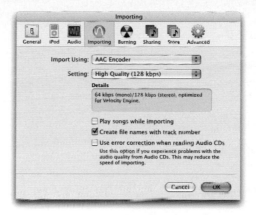

Converting songs to fit on the iPod Shuffle

The Shuffle plays tracks in the AAC, MP3, Audible, and WAV formats, but it can't play the super-large, uncompressed AIFF or Apple Lossless formats. This doesn't mean that you can't ever play them, though—you just have to convert them to the AAC format first. And best of all, iTunes will do it for you!

Just plug in the iPod Shuffle, open the Preferences box, and click the iPod tab or icon. Check the box next to "Convert higher bit rate songs to 128kbps AAC for this iPod" and click OK. This sends an AAC copy of the song to the Shuffle but leaves the original AIFF or Apple Lossless file just the way it was back in your iTunes Library.

If you have MP3 files encoded at higher bit rates (like 160 or 192kbps) that you want to transfer to the Shuffle, you might want to turn off this setting, though. Those files will also get converted to the 128kbps AAC format as well and may not sound as good as you remember them.

Getting Started

iTunes

Filling Shuffle
with Music

Playing with
Playlists

Pocket USB
Drive

Cool Stuff for
iPod Shuffle

More Shuffle
Resources

iPod
Shuffle
Fan Book

24

Fun things to do with your iTunes library

Although may it seem like a simple little music-ripping and iPod-loading program, iTunes is also a super-powerful database that you can use to keep track of thousands and thousands of songs in your digital music collection.

Here are some of the things you can do to a song just by clicking on it, choosing File→Get Info and clicking the Info and Options tabs:

Rate it You can give your songs a rating of one to five stars, which comes in handy when you want to have all your top-rated songs get on board the iPod Shuffle first.

Equalize it Different kinds of music sound better with different equalizer settings, and iTunes has plenty of settings to choose from in the pop-up tab in the bottom of the box.

Categorize it You can put songs into the different genres that the database chooses, or make up whole genres of your own like Asian Rap or Broadway Showtunes.

You can edit all the tracks on the album at once or just pick a few tracks to edit. Select several songs by clicking on the first one you want to edit, hold the down the Shift key, and then click on the last song you want to change. After the songs are highlighted, select File→Get Info and you can change the genre, album title, and other information for all the songs you've selected.

Editing song tag information

Everyone makes mistakes and sometimes there's a typo in a song title you downloaded from the Internet database. Or maybe you just want to edit the song information yourself. You can do this easily by clicking the song once and choosing File→Get Info. Now you can type what you want for the title or album.

Visuals and album artwork

The iTunes program can look as good on your computer as it sounds, too. If you want to zone out and watch some dreamy, floating patterns onscreen, click the Visualizer button in the bottom corner of the window or choose Visualizer→Turn Visualizer On. (Turn it off from the same menu.) You can make the visuals take up the whole screen or just stay within the same menu.

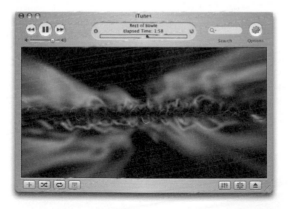

Getting Started

iTunes

Filling Shuffle
with Music

Playing with
Playlists

Pocket USB
Drive

Cool Stuff for
iPod Shuffle

More Shuffle
Resources

You can jazz up your iTunes display even more when you are rocking out at your desk with album artwork in your iTunes window. Any track you buy from the iTunes Music Store will have an electronic picture of the album cover attached to it that you can see in the Artwork pane of the iTunes window.

You can also add your own digital photos or album cover artwork to tracks you rip yourself in iTunes. Just drag-and-drop a picture into the empty artwork pane to add it.

Many creative programmers have written software to make adding artwork even easier. If you have a Macintosh, try Clutter (*http://sprote.com/clutter*), a program that

snags artwork for any album you're playing and lets you add it to iTunes with File→Copy Cover to iTunes.

To get album artwork for their songs, Windows folks can use the iTunes Art Importer (*www.yvg.com/ itunesartimporter.shtml*).

There's also a Web-based service called art4iTunes (*www.art4itunes.com*) that snags album covers for you. You just need to export the desired song list in the plain-text format from iTunes (choose File→Export Song List) and upload the file using a form on the web site. The web site rounds up the appropriate album covers from your playlist and displays them so you can then drag-and-drop them right into iTunes.

Internet radio

When you're connected to the Internet, you can even listen to online radio stations with iTunes. Just click the Radio icon in the Source list and select the station you want to hear from the big list in the display window.

Once you've listen to all the stations listed in iTunes, check out the offerings on the Web. There are more radio stations at sites such as *www.live365.com* and *www.shoutcast.com* and you can play them in iTunes when you click the link to listen.

If you really love radio, check out Griffin Technology's RadioSHARK, a festive fin-shaped attachment that plugs into your computer's USB port. With the RadioSHARK, you listen and record AM/FM radio broadcasts even if you're not at the computer. It's also easy to copy the recorded files to your iPod Shuffle by using iTunes. The RadioSHARK sells for $70 at *www.griffintechnology.com/ products/radioshark*.

radioSHARK

Getting Started

iTunes

Filling Shuffle
with Music

Playing with
Playlists

Pocket USB
Drive

Cool Stuff for
iPod Shuffle

More Shuffle
Resources

It's possible to save music streams to your computer's hard drive, although it might be considered copyright infringement by some legal authorities. Programs like RadioLover (*www.bitcartel.com/radiolover*) and Streamripper X (*http://streamripperx.sourceforge.net*), for Mac OS X or Audiolib MP3 Recorder (at *www.audiolib.com/recorder*) and Rip-Cast (*www.xoteck.com/ripcast*) for Windows let you save radio streams as MP3 files.

The iTunes Music Store

A whole world of possibilities—and more than a million songs—all await you in the iTunes Music Store, and all you need to do to get there is click the Music Store icon in your iTunes Source list and let your Internet connection do the driving. Inside the store, you can buy songs and albums, watch music videos and movie trailers, see what people are listening to around the country, and a whole lot more.

Just about every song in the Store is 99 cents and you can hear a 30-second preview of each track by double-clicking on it to see if you like it. Use the Search box to seek out specific song titles or click around through different genres until you find something you want to buy.

To buy music, you have to have an Apple Account with a valid credit card number. To set up an Apple Account, click the Sign In button on the right side of the iTunes window. The Sign In box pops up and you can click the Create New Account button to get your Apple Account started. You need to set up a username and password, and provide a credit card for billing.

Sign In to download music from the iTunes Music Store
To create an Apple Account, click Create New Account.

(Create New Account)

If you have an Apple Account (from the Apple Store or .Mac, for example), enter your Apple ID and password. Otherwise, if you are an AOL member, enter your AOL screen name and password.

Apple ID:
Example: steve@mac.com

Password:
(Forgot Password?)

(Cancel) (Sign In)

You can also use a PayPal account for billing and if you already have an America Online account, you can sign into the iTunes Music Store right away using your AOL Screen Name and password. If you choose to use your AOL name for iTunes, just set up your AOL Wallet (Keyword: AOL Wallet) to handle your bills for online shopping.

Getting Started

iTunes

Filling Shuffle
with Music

Playing with
Playlists

Pocket USB
Drive

Cool Stuff for
iPod Shuffle

More Shuffle
Resources

Buying songs from the iTunes Music Store

After you have your Apple Account set up, you're ready to buy some songs. The main page of the iTunes Music Store is clearly laid out with links and menus to help you find the type of music you're looking for, from alternative rock to zydeco tunes in the World music category.

When you find a song or album you want to purchase, click the Buy Song or Buy Album button. Buying music is much quicker if you have a broadband connection because the songs can just slide down the wire with your cable or DSL modem, but if you have a dial-up Internet account, you can turn on the Shopping Cart feature in the Store preferences to download all the songs at the very end of your shopping session.

To turn on the Shopping Cart, choose iTunes→Preferences→Store on the Mac or Edit→Preferences→ Store in Windows and click the button next to "Buy using a Shopping Cart."

Songs you have bought show up in the Purchased Music playlist in the iTunes Source list as well as in their natural artist and album lists. From there, you can copy them over to your iPod Shuffle, as you'll learn in the next chapter.

You can play iTunes Music Store music on five different computers, but you have to *authorize* each machine to play them by typing in your Apple Account name and password the first time you try to play a purchased song.

Once you reach your five allotted Macs or PCs, you won't be able to play the music on any more machines until you *deauthorize* one of the others by choosing Advanced → Deauthorize Computer.

Buying and listening to audiobooks

The iTunes Music Store sells more than 5,000 audiobooks right there in its window, but you can find many more from a company called Audible (*www.audible.com*). Audible files come in their own *.aa* format, and you have to have a password to play them on your computer. You can play Audible books and shows on your iPod Shuffle, but you need to have the Shuffle set to Play In Order. If you use the Shuffle setting, your songs will get mixed in with your Audible content.

To buy spoken-word content from Audible, you need to set up an account on the company's web site. The company offers subscription plans for people who like to listen to a lot of audiobooks.

If you choose to sign up for the $15-a-month BasicListener program you get one recorded book a month, plus a daily, weekly, or monthly magazine or radio show. Audible. com has many recorded periodicals to choose from on its web site.

There's also a PreminumListener plan that gets you two audio book titles, (but no periodical subscriptions) for about $20 a month. You can hear free samples of most files on the site before you buy.

Getting Started

iTunes

Filling Shuffle
with Music

Playing with
Playlists

Pocket USB
Drive

Cool Stuff for
iPod Shuffle

More Shuffle
Resources

iPod
Shuffle
Fan Book

You can also skip the monthly-plan business and just buy the books you want for a flat fee. Prices vary, but the audio file usually costs less than the heavy bookstore version and fits better on your iPod Shuffle.

The Audible site has full instructions for setting up an iPod to play the downloaded audiobooks and other content with iTunes.

Gym workouts for your iPod Shuffle

With its small, lightweight body, the iPod Shuffle is perfect for working out at the gym, and it can also withstand more bouncing around than a regular iPod. You can rerip your favorite workout CDs to load onto your Shuffle or download workout routines in MP3 format from places like *www.mp3gym.com* to really feel the burn.

Filling the iPod Shuffle with Music

Getting Started

iTunes

Filling Shuffle
with Music

Playing with
Playlists

Pocket USB
Drive

Cool Stuff for
iPod Shuffle

More Shuffle
Resources

Getting ready to move your music

The first two chapters of this book explained how to work the iPod Shuffle and how to make digital music files in iTunes. Now it's time to put it all together so you can load up your Shuffle and get going.

The world is full of choices, and here are some more of them. You can have iTunes decide what music to put on your iPod Shuffle, or you can personally choose the tracks you want to take with you.

If you have been using iTunes for longer than a month, you probably already have hundreds of songs on your hard drive. You obviously can't fit them all on your little 512-megabyte or 1 gigabyte iPod Shuffle, but if you don't want to spend the time picking out music, you can have the computer do it for you.

But to get any sort of music on the iPod Shuffle, you need to start by making sure it's plugged into the computer and visible in the iTunes Source list. You'll see a little tiny Shuffle icon in the list, labeled with whatever you named it when you set it up. Now you are ready to decide how you want to fill it up.

Automatic music fill-up with iTunes

One fast, easy, and fun way to put songs on your iPod Shuffle is to *Autofill* it. As soon as you plug in the Shuffle and iTunes sees it, you'll see a small panel at the bottom of the iTunes window. This is the Autofill area, and one click of the Autofill button makes iTunes fill up your iPod Shuffle to the brim with randomly selected music from your iTunes library.

If you want to narrow down your selections instead of autofilling from all over your giant music library, you can use the pop-up menu to select a certain playlist as the source of your Autofilling. There are also check boxes in the Autofill area to make iTunes look for songs that you've given the highest star ratings or to just pick them totally randomly— which can be a lot of fun if you have a wide variety of music in your collection.

Once you've Autofilled for the first time and then return for another batch of songs, you can check the box next to "Replace all songs when autofilling" to have iTunes erase the first group of songs off the Shuffle and substitute them with new songs. This way you won't know what to expect next time you play your Shuffle. If you don't check the box to replace the songs, iTunes will just keep autofilling from the selected source until the Shuffle is maxed out with music.

If you've got iTunes Music Store songs in your selected source, make sure your computer is authorized to play them, or iTunes will complain and say it couldn't move unauthorized tracks that were selected for Autofilling.

Getting Started

iTunes

**Filling Shuffle
with Music**

Playing with
Playlists

Pocket USB
Drive

Cool Stuff for
iPod Shuffle

More Shuffle
Resources

Once iTunes has filled up the Shuffle, you'll see the "OK to disconnect" message in the iTunes status display. Click the Eject button next to your Shuffle's icon in the Source list to disconnect it and then unplug the player from the computer.

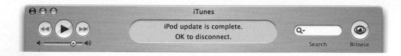

Adding the music yourself

Some people don't like surprises or want to carry specific music with them. If you're one of these folks, you can take over the music-loading from iTunes and put exactly want you want on your iPod Shuffle.

Plug your Shuffle into the USB port and wait for it to show up in iTunes. When you see its icon in the Source list, click on your Library icon and drag song titles from the Browser or Song Display window and drop them onto the iPod Shuffle icon to add them. You'll see a progress bar at the top of the iTunes Status window showing you the songs being added. You can drag whole albums and playlists onto the iPod Shuffle icon, too.

When you've clicked on the Shuffle's icon in the Source list, you can arrange individual songs into the sequence you wish to hear them. The information down at the bottom of the iTunes window tells you how much space you're taking on your Shuffle so you know when you're close to filling it all the way up.

You can also mix and match your song-loading methods. Start by dragging a few favorite playlists over to the Shuffle, and then click Autofill to finish the job. Just make sure the "Replace all songs when autofilling" box isn't turned on or iTunes will totally erase all those tracks you manually added.

One iPod Shuffle, one computer

With regular iPods you can use the manual update option to collect songs from multiple computers, such as your work and your home machines. However, the stubborn Shuffle works with only one Mac or PC at a time—it won't let you add music from different machines without erasing everything you've got on your Shuffle.

Adding music without the Shuffle connected

Once you've plugged your iPod Shuffle into the computer to add songs, you can set it up so that you can add music to it—even if you don't have it plugged in. There's a setting in the Preferences box that lets you always see your Shuffle's icon in iTunes.

Select the Shuffle's icon in the iTunes Source list. Click the iPod icon button at the bottom of the iTunes window to open the Preferences box and check the box for "Keep this iPod in the Source list," before clicking OK.

Now your Shuffle's icon will always be there for you, even when you accidentally leave the real Shuffle in your locker. You can drag over songs from iTunes to it just like it was

really there, and the next time you plug in the actual Shuffle to the computer, it syncs up all those new songs you added in its absence.

When you drag over a song to the Virtual Shuffle, a small gray dot appears next to its name to let you know that it's scheduled to transfer to the iPod Shuffle the next time you plug in the player.

Getting Started

iTunes

Filling Shuffle
with Music

Playing with
Playlists

Pocket USB
Drive

Cool Stuff for
iPod Shuffle

More Shuffle
Resources

Deleting songs from the iPod Shuffle

When you've tired of the Shuffle's songs, you can easily take off the old ones and put on some fresh tunes.

If you are letting iTunes fill up your Shuffle for you, plug it in and click the Autofill button again. Make sure the "Replace all songs when autofilling" box is checked.

If you manually add songs to your player, connect it and click the Shuffle's icon in the Source list to call up its contents in the main iTunes window. Click the song titles you want to remove and hit the Delete key.

Adding audio books

The iPod Shuffle isn't just for music. It can store and play your favorite audio books from Audible and iTunes, too.

You can't use the Autofill function, though—you have to manually add the audio books to the iPod Shuffle by dragging them over to the Shuffle icon yourself.

Make sure the switch on the back of the iPod Shuffle is set to Play In Order, too, and not to Shuffle, because when the Shuffle setting is on, the player skips audio books and just plays music tracks.

iPod
Shuffle
Fan Book

Playing with Playlists

Getting Started

iTunes

Filling Shuffle
with Music

Playing with
Playlists

Pocket USB
Drive

Cool Stuff for
iPod Shuffle

More Shuffle
Resources

The wonderful world of playlists

A *playlist* is a list of songs that *you* think should go together, and not what songs a record company or a radio station or a DJ in a club thinks should be grouped together. With iTunes, making playlists is easy—all you need are a few clicks or commands and an opinion about what you want to hear.

You can have lots of different playlists in iTunes and copy them over to your iPod Shuffle. You can design a sequence of dance songs for that big party you're having this weekend and then put that same playlist in your Shuffle to use as your workout music at the gym. Or maybe you'd like a quieter mix of different classical music numbers to play when you're studying or reading the paper.

Once you make a playlist, you can change it around, add new songs to it, mix it all up with your Shuffle, or when you're tired of it—delete it and make a brand new one to match your mood that day.

Making a new playlist

There are many ways to make a playlist in iTunes. One way is to press Command-N (Mac) or Ctrl+N (Windows) on the keyboard. You can also choose File→New Playlist or click the + button below the Source area of the iTunes window.

All fresh new playlists start out named Untitled Playlist, but you can click on the title and type in your own name for it like Party Mix or Yoga Practice or House Cleaning Jam. The playlists alphabetize themselves in the Source window so you can quickly find the one you want to play.

Now you're ready to add some songs!

If this is your first playlist, opening the playlist into its own window may make it easier for you to see what's going on. To do so, double-click the new playlist's icon in the Source list, which opens a window next to your main iTunes window. From here, drag the song titles from your iTunes library over to the new playlist window.

Another way to add songs to a playlist is by dragging them from the main iTunes window to the playlist's icon in the Source list.

You can also make a new playlist by scrolling through a big list of songs, selecting tracks as you go by Command-clicking on the Mac or Control-clicking in Windows, and then

choosing File→New Playlist From Selection. A new playlist filled with the songs you've just selected will appear, ready for you to play

Playlists don't fill up your hard drive, either. When you drag a song title onto a playlist, you don't *copy* the song; you're just giving iTunes instructions about where to find the files. In essence, you're creating an *alias* or *shortcut* of the original. You can have the same song on several different playlists.

Changing songs around on a playlist

If you change your mind about the order of the tunes you've selected for a playlist, just drag the song titles up or down within the playlist window to reorder them.

You can also drag more songs into a playlist, or delete the titles from the list if you find your playlist has gotten too long or boring. Click the song in the playlist window and hit Delete or Backspace to get rid of it. When iTunes asks you to confirm your decision, click Yes.

Deleting a song from a playlist doesn't erase it from your music library—it just removes the title from your *playlist*. Only pressing Delete or Backspace when the *Library* icon is selected gets rid of the song for good.

Getting Started

iTunes

Filling Shuffle
with Music

Playing with
Playlists

Pocket USB
Drive

Cool Stuff for
iPod Shuffle

More Shuffle
Resources

Sample playlists

Playlists are anything you want them to be, but if you are stuck for ideas, The iPod Shuffle Fan Book has a few suggestions to get you rolling. All the songs are just a few clicks away inside the iTunes Music Store.

Classic American Rock

An exuberant new form of music called rock and roll first burst onto the pop charts in the mid-1950s and caught the ears of teenagers around the country. American rock music fused country and R&B styles to create an infectious blend of energetic rhythms underneath lyrics that had a lot to do about love, life, and having a good time. From the Southern sounds of Elvis Presley to the steady Motown beats of Martha Reeves to the West Coast pop of the Beach Boys and Janis Joplin, classic American rock reflects the diversity of America itself.

Rock Around the Clock	Bill Haley & His Comets
Jailhouse Rock	Elvis Presley
Peggy Sue	Buddy Holly
Come Go With Me	The Del Vikings
Fingertips, Pt. 2 (Live)	Stevie Wonder
My Boyfriend's Back	The Angels
Dancing in the Street	Martha Reeves & The Vandellas
Like A Rolling Stone	Bob Dylan
Respect	Aretha Franklin
California Dreamin'	The Mamas & The Papas
Good Vibrations	The Beach Boys
Mrs. Robinson	Simon & Garfunkel
Sittin' on the Dock of the Bay	Otis Redding
Proud Mary	Creedence Clearwater Revival
Me and Bobby McGee	Janis Joplin

iPod
Shuffle
Fan Book

The Interstate Car Trip Mix

Music and driving go together for decades (the first car radio appeared in 1929, after all) and the rhythms of the road have no doubt inspired many a melody. All the songs in this mostly country-rock mix are about driving down life's highways, whether they be concrete or abstract. From Willie Nelson's anxiousness to "get on the road again" to Dave Dudley's tired trucker singing about his past six days of constant driving, the songs of the Interstate troubadours can keep you going.

On the Road Again	Willie Nelson
East Bound and Down	Jerry Reed
Long Time Gone	The Dixie Chicks
Traveling Again (Traveling I)	Dar Williams
King of the Road	Roger Miller
Leaving Louisiana in the Broad Daylight	Emmylou Harris
Highway 61	Bob Dylan
Road to Nowhere	Talking Heads
Nowhere Road	Steve Earle
Listen to the Radio	Nanci Griffith
Baby Driver	Simon & Garfunkel
Drivin' My Life Away	Eddie Rabbit
Running on Empty	Jackson Browne
I've Been Everywhere	Johnny Cash
Six Days on the Road	Dave Dudley

Getting Started

iTunes

Filling Shuffle
with Music

Playing with
Playlists

Pocket USB
Drive

Cool Stuff for
iPod Shuffle

More Shuffle
Resources

The Moody Mix

Music can affect your emotional state and a number of great songs were obviously written by people in sad or bad moods. Love, loss, and loss of love are often the subjects of the world's best moody songs. These songs span different styles of music from the twangy heartache of Patsy Cline to the modern soul of Alicia Keys, and the somber lyrics may help put things in perspective and let you know you're not alone.

Sad Songs (Say So Much)	Elton John
I Fall to Pieces	Patsy Cline
I'm So Lonesome I Could Cry	Hank Williams
Man of Constant Sorrow	The Stanley Brothers
When Will I Be Loved	Linda Ronstadt
Tracks of My Tears	Smokey Robinson & The Miracles
Hallelujah	Leonard Cohen
I Can't Make You Love Me	Bonnie Raitt
Verdi Cries	10,000 Maniacs
Misguided Angel	Cowboy Junkies
Then Came Lo Mein	Robert Earl Keen
Poor Poor Pitiful Me	Warren Zevon
If I Ain't Got You	Alicia Keys
Black and Blue	The Gene Harris Quartet

iPod
Shuffle
Fan Book

Happy Fun Songs

Once you've had your festival of sad songs, there are plenty of happy tunes to improve your mood. Bouncy beats and joyful lyrics go well together for gym workouts, parties, or plain old feeling good. Who can be sad with the Godfather of Soul, Moby's electronic euphoria, and the sheer megawatt vocal power of Aretha Franklin and Annie Lennox blasting through your iPod Shuffle headphones?

I Got You (I Feel Good)	James Brown
Get the Party Started	Pink
Honey	Moby
Twist and Shout	Salt-n-Pepa
Good Lovin'	The Rascals
I Want You Back	Jackson 5
Girls Just Wanna Have Fun	Cyndi Lauper
Walk This Way	Run DMC/Aerosmith
Let's Go Crazy	Prince
Love Shack	The B-52s
All Star	Smash Mouth
Living La Vida Loca	Ricky Martin
Sisters Are Doin' It For Themselves	Aretha Franklin & Eurythmics
Jerk It Out	Caesars
Word Up!	Cameo
Hey Ya!	Outkast

Getting Started

iTunes

Filling Shuffle
with Music

Playing with
Playlists

Pocket USB
Drive

Cool Stuff for
iPod Shuffle

More Shuffle
Resources

Deleting a playlist

When you get tired of a playlist or what to clean up your iTunes Source list because there are too many items in there, you can delete the playlists you don't want anymore. To delete a playlist, click it in the Source list and press Delete (Backspace).

Don't worry, you're not deleting your actual song files. Deleting a playlist just zaps the list itself, not all the stored songs you had in it. The song files themselves are still in your iTunes Music folder.

Shuffling songs in iTunes

If you are stuck at your desk and can't run around listening to music, you can make iTunes act like your iPod Shuffle and mix up your songs with the click of a button.

Click the familiar crossed-arrows Shuffle button at the bottom of the iTunes window. You'll hear your playlist songs in a random order. Click the Shuffle button again to unshuffle your music.

Getting smart with Smart Playlists

Just as you can have iTunes shuffle your songs like it was a big iPod Shuffle, you can also have the program compose playlists all by itself for you. All you have to do is give iTunes some guidelines about what kinds of songs to use and it goes shopping through your music library to come up with its own mix for you.

iPod
Shuffle
Fan Book

These computer-composed playlists are called *Smart Playlists*. The Smart Playlist even keeps tabs on the songs that come and go from your library and adjusts itself on the fly to keep up with your musical inspirations and acquisitions.

You might tell one Smart Playlist to assemble an hour's worth of songs from the 1990's that you've rated higher than four stars or make another one of tracks sung only by Ella Fitzgerald, Billie Holiday, and Lena Horne —and nobody else. These Smart Playlists can be dragged over to your iPod Shuffle like any other old playlist for you to listen to on the go.

Making a Smart Playlist

To start a Smart Playlist in iTunes, press Option+ Command+N (Mac) or Ctrl+Alt+N (Windows) or choose File→New Smart Playlist.

You can also make a new Smart Playlist with the buttons at the bottom of the iTunes window. When you press Option (Mac) or Shift (Windows), the + button for Add New Playlist at the bottom of the iTunes window turns into a gear icon. Click the gear button to get a new Smart Playlist to appear in the Source list, all ready for you to set up. (Smart Play-

lists have a purple gear-shaped icon next to the name in the Source list, while a regular playlist has a blue icon with a music note icon in it.)

When the Smart Playlist box opens, you are ready to tell iTunes what you want to hear.

Getting Started

iTunes

Filling Shuffle
with Music

Playing with
Playlists

Pocket USB
Drive

Cool Stuff for
iPod Shuffle

More Shuffle
Resources

Type in the names of the artists you want to hear and have iTunes leave off the ones you're not in the mood for, grab songs that only fall within a certain genre or year, and so on. You can make a Smart Playlist using information from any field in the song's tag, like a collection of every tune in your library that's track 13 on an album or any song that has the word "love" in the title.

Click the plus button (+) to add more data fields to the Smart Playlists box and shape your musical vision every further. Check the "Live updating" to keep the playlist updated as your collection changes.

A Smart Playlist is a conversation between you and iTunes: You tell it what you want in as much detail as you want, and the program responds back with what it thinks you want to hear. Once you give it some boundaries, iTunes drills down through the current contents of your music library and creates the new playlist for you.

Finding playlist inspiration on the Web

Playlists can become an obsession, and if you want to learn more about making them—or what goes into a good mix—several web sites are dedicated to the topic.

If you're a fan of the Smart Playlists feature in iTunes, check out the scene at *www.smartplaylists.com*. You'll find many Smart Playlists experts exchanging tips, tricks, and tales as well as sharing their thoughts about Apple, iTunes, and other subjects.

The Art of the Mix site (*www.artofthemix.org*) is a web-based community of folks dedicated to making exciting and inventive playlists. You can see samples of everything from world music mixes to song collections devoted to music for moody teenagers.

iPod
Shuffle
Fan Book

Publishing your own playlists (iMixes)

An *iMix* is a playlist that you publish on the iTunes Music Store, so everyone shopping in Apple's music emporium can see your expert playlist composition. You can name your iMix, write your own liner notes explaining your inspiration for making it, and put it out there for the iTunes world to see.

The first step in making an iMix is signing into your Music Store account. Then in the iTunes Source list, select the playlist you want to publish. Be warned that if the playlist has any songs that Apple *doesn't* sell, they'll get knocked off the list—which may ruin your very special music mix.

When you click the playlist, a gray arrow appears next to its title. Click the arrow to begin the publishing process (or choose File→Publish Playlist to Music Store).

In the warning box, click Publish (and turn on "Do not show this message again" if you are tired of iTunes warning boxes popping up at you).

On the next screen, name your iMix and add your thoughts on making it.

Getting Started

iTunes

Filling Shuffle
with Music

Playing with
Playlists

Pocket USB
Drive

Cool Stuff for
iPod Shuffle

More Shuffle
Resources

iPod
Shuffle
Fan Book

50

Finally, in the iMix window, click Publish. Now other people can see your playlist, rate it, be inspired by it, or buy the songs for themselves after you've shown them how good the music fits together thanks to your brilliance.

You can tell all your friends about your new iMix, too. Click the Tell a Friend button on your new iMix page and iTunes sends an announcement by email, complete with album-cover art. Apple will send you an email message congratulating you on your successful iMixing along with a link for your iMix. The Store keeps iMixes on its site for a year.

You can also email a friend a direct link to your brand new iMix, or one that you think is cool in the Store. Control-click or right-click the playlist's icon on the iMix page and, from the shortcut menu, choose "Copy iTunes Music Store URL." Next, create a new message in your email program and paste in the link you just copied.

Discovering iTunes Essentials

Learning about new kinds of music can be a lot of fun, but because there's so much music out there in the world, you may not know where to start. The iTunes Music Store can help you explore new sonic frontiers with its iTunes Essentials playlists, which are song collections designed by music experts at the Store.

These Essentials playlists are grouped by artist, genre, or even topic, like Sunday Morning Chill Out for those mellow weekend mornings or Latin Pop, highlighting the best songs and singers in the Latin American music scene. You can find introductory samplers in funk, punk, hip-hop, disco, folk, bluegrass, reggae, salsa, techno, and dozens of other musical styles.

Each Essentials playlist is composed of three levels: The Basics, Next Steps, and Deep Cuts. If you find you like all the songs on the Basics level (which are typically the biggest hits of an artist or genre), you can explore the Next Steps, which are usually popular, but lesser-known songs in the subject area. If you find you really love the music, you can go even further into it with the Deep Cuts selections that highlight more obscure material.

To find the iTunes Essentials, go to the Music Store's main page, click the link for iTunes Essentials, and select the topic you're interested in. If you like the song samples, you can buy a whole iTunes Essentials playlist with one click or just pick the tracks you like the best for 99 cents each.

Say you wanted to learn more about jazz music, which has a long and complex history. The Jazz 101 playlist in the iTunes Essentials area offers these 25 songs as a Basics starter set that highlights many of the pivotal performers and performances in the genre, all neatly collected in one place and available for purchase with a single mouse click:

So What	Miles Davis
Take Five	The Dave Brubeck Quartet
God Bless the Child	Billie Holiday
Take the "A" Train	Duke Ellington & His Famous Orchestra
Koko	Charlie Parker
Goodbye Pork Pie Hat	Charles Mingus
Impressions	John Coltrane
Heebie Jeebies	Louis Armstrong & His Hot Fives
My Funny Valentine	Chet Baker
Straight, No Chaser	Thelonious Monk
Desafinado (Off Key)	Charlie Byrd & Stan Getz

Getting Started

iTunes

Filling Shuffle
with Music

Playing with
Playlists

Pocket USB
Drive

Cool Stuff for
iPod Shuffle

More Shuffle
Resources

Body and Soul	Coleman Hawkins & Billy Byers and His Orchestra
Sing, Sing, Sing	Benny Goodman and His Orchestra
Jumpin' at the Woodside (1938 Version)	Count Basie & Quincy Jones & His Orchestra
Flying Home	Benny Goodman, Charlie Christian & The Benny Goodman Sextet
A Night in Tunisia	Dizzy Gillespie & His Orchestra
How High the Moon (1st Take)	Ella Fitzgerald
Maiden Voyage	Herbie Hancock
Waltz for Debby	Bill Evans
Lester Leaps In	Count Basie & The Kansas City 7
Honeysuckle Rose	Django Reinhardt & Stéphane Grappelli
Bouncing with Bud	Bud Powell
Tiger Rag	Art Tatum
Sweet Lorraine	The Nat "King" Cole Trio
Three O'Clock in the Morning	Dexter Gordon

If you like what you hear, you can go back for more by clicking the tabs for The Next Steps and Deep Cuts. There's also a tab to click if you want to buy all three levels of an Essentials mix, but be prepared for a charge of $75 or so on your credit if you buy the whole shebang at once.

Celebrity playlists

Just like you can get ideas for cool outfits and personal fashion from what you see actors wearing in movies and on television, you can get ideas for your own playlists from what your favorite bands, singers, or other performers are listening to in the Celebrity Playlists area of the iTunes Music Store.

Click the Celebrity Playlists link on the main page of the Music Store to get started. Once you get there, you'll see more than 160 personal playlists created by various entertainers from around the music and movie worlds. Here, you can find out what Kanye West, Tom Petty, Sleater-Kinney, and other famous people are listening to. Many contributors even took the time to write up a short note explaining why they liked these particular songs together.

You can get all sorts of ideas from the Celebrity Playlists area. For example, King Britt, a music producer and DJ, compiled an eclectic mix of songs that have influenced him, and provided detailed notes on why each particular song is on his playlist:

Nature's Way	This Mortal Coil
Have You Ever Been (To Electric Ladyland)	The Jimi Hendrix Experience
Come Live With Me	Dorothy Ashby
Us and Them	Pink Floyd
Close the Door	Rufus & Chaka Khan
For Love	Sylk 130 & Grover Washington, Jr.

Getting Started

iTunes

Filling Shuffle
with Music

Playing with
Playlists

Pocket USB
Drive

Cool Stuff for
iPod Shuffle

More Shuffle
Resources

iPod
Shuffle
Fan Book

Other Side of the Game	Erykah Badu
I Miss You (Double Rub Part One-Sunshine Mix)	Björk
Feet-Like Fins	Cocteau Twins
This Is Not America	David Bowie, featuring the Pat Metheny Group
I Want You for Myself	George Duke
If I Can't Have You	Yvonne Elliman
Season's Change (Philharmonix Mix)	Sylk 130
Appointment at the Fat Clinic	Digable Planets

But the Celebrity Playlists area is not just for music professionals. Jennifer Garner, the star of TV's *Alias* and the action film *Elektra,* posted her own workout playlist:

The Way You Move	Outkast & Sleepy Brown
Daughters	John Mayer
Fallin'	Alicia Keys
What You Waiting For?	Gwen Stefani
Crazy in Love	Beyoncé
Rock Your Body	Justin Timberlake
This Love	Maroon 5
Get the Party Started	Pink
Yeah!	Usher
Lose My Breath	Destiny's Child

Even if you don't like all the songs, you might be able to get some inspiration for your own playlists just by seeing what other people you like have on their iPods.

Burning a playlist to CD or DVD

In addition to loading them up on your iPod Shuffle, another easy way to take your favorite iTunes playlists with you it to burn them to a CD that you can listen to in the car or on a stereo. Your iTunes program makes it very easy to burn different kinds of discs.

One popular type of disc is the standard *Audio CD* that just about every home and car stereo CD player can read. All you need is a CD burner that meets Apple's specifications (there's a list at *www.apple.com/support/itunes*) and some blank CDs, which are very inexpensive these days.

Another type of disc that is becoming very common is the *MP3 CD*, which is a regular compact disc filled up with songs in the MP3 format instead of the usual big files used for standard audio CDs. You can easily store 10 to 12 hours of MP3 music on one single MP3 CD, but not all CD players can read these discs. Most computers, however, can read them just fine.

Getting Started

iTunes

Filling Shuffle
with Music

Playing with
Playlists

Pocket USB
Drive

Cool Stuff for
iPod Shuffle

More Shuffle
Resources

If you have purchased a lot of music from the iTunes Music Store or spent hours ripping your favorite CDs for use on your iPod Shuffle, you may want to consider making the third type of disc sometime, too. This is the *Data CD or DVD*, and it saves copies of your song files in their MP3 or AAC or other iTunes-friendly format. You can't play this type of disc on the car stereo, but if your computer crashes, you can restore your lost music files from this helpful CD or DVD.

To pick your CD format, choose iTunes→Preferences→Burning on the Mac or Edit→ Preferences→Burning on a Windows PC and click the button next to the type of disc you want to make. (If your playlist is too long to fit on the disc in the format you want, iTunes will let you know before you get started with the burning process.)

Now you're ready to make a CD of your favorite music in three easy steps:

❶ Click on the iTunes the playlist you want to burn and make sure it's exactly how you want to record it.

❷ Click the Burn Disc button at the top-right corner of the iTunes window.

❸ Insert a blank CD when iTunes asks you for one and click the Burn Disc button again after the program accepts the disc.

While you wait, iTunes will cook up your CD and give you a message when it's all done. Now you can eject the disc and go play it loud as you drive down the highway or crank it up on a boom box while you hang out with friends at the beach.

iPod
Shuffle
Fan Book

Making CD covers

If you want to give your iTunes mixes to friends, you can make a nice CD cover right in iTunes that includes album art from any of your iTunes Music Store purchases or your own photos that you've added to your music files. You can also print out a straightforward list of songs or the names of the albums that the songs in the mix were from.

To get to all of these options, click the iTunes playlist you want to use and choose File→ Print. You'll see lots of options that you can select to jazz up that CD you just burned.

iPod Shuffle as Pocket USB Drive

5

Getting Started

iTunes

Filling Shuffle
with Music

Playing with
Playlists

**Pocket USB
Drive**

Cool Stuff for
iPod Shuffle

More Shuffle
Resources

Using the iPod Shuffle to carry files

The iPod Shuffle is not just a music player! It can serve double duty as one of those tiny USB flash-memory drives that you copy and cart your data files around from computer to computer.

Once you configure the Shuffle properly, you can drag word-processing documents, PowerPoint presentations, digital photographs, and other files too big to email onto the Shuffle's hard drive. When you plug it into another computer's USB port, you can then drag copies of those files onto the new machine, saving you lots of time and download-ing boredom.

If you're job hunting, putting a PDF copy of your resume on your Shuffle means that you'll be able to print it out while on the go and apply for your dream job from just about anywhere. Resumes also have your name, phone number, and email address on them, so if you happen to lose your Shuffle and an honest person finds it, they might be able to use this information to contact you and arrange for its safe return.

iPod
Shuffle
Fan Book

Configuring the Shuffle in iTunes

To set up the iPod Shuffle to work overtime as a pocket USB drive, connect it to the computer and open its preferences box by clicking on its icon in the Source list and then clicking on the iPod icon in the bottom of the iTunes window.

In the iPod Shuffle preferences area, check the box next to "Enable disk use." Move the little slider bar along to split up your Shuffle's space between music and data. Remember, if you take more room for data storage, you have less room for music, so think carefully about how you want to divide up your 512 megabytes or 1 gigabyte of Shuffle space.

While you're in the Preferences box, you may want to turn off the setting that tells the computer to open iTunes every time you plug in the Shuffle, especially if you plan to plug in

the Shuffle on several different computers to move data files around. By turning off the automatic iTunes-opening feature, you avoid the alert box about the iPod being linked to another iTunes Library that pops up every time you connect the Shuffle to a computer other than the one you have your music stored on.

There may come a time when you need more room for music or vice versa, and when that time comes, go back to the iPod preferences box and readjust the slider.

Getting Started

iTunes

Filling Shuffle
with Music

Playing with
Playlists

**Pocket USB
Drive**

Cool Stuff for
iPod Shuffle

More Shuffle
Resources

iPod
Shuffle
Fan Book

62

Moving files to and from the Shuffle

Once you set up your Shuffle's preferences, you'll see it show up on the
computer as another external drive,
either in the My Computer area on a
Windows PC, or on the desktop and
list of drives connected to a Mac.
Once you see the Shuffle's icon, you
can drag-and-drop files onto it, just
like the music player was any old
generic flash drive, Zip disk, external
hard drive, old-fashioned floppy disk,
or any other form of portable media.

If you want to permanently delete a data
file from your iPod Shuffle, drag the un-
wanted document to your Trash or Recy-
cle Bin and then empty it.

Properly disconnecting the Shuffle from the computer

Once you configure the Shuffle to be an external drive, the computer considers your little white music player to be like any other external device that must be correctly disconnected before can you unplug it. (Just yanking the Shuffle out of the USB port before the computer is ready to let go of the drive can cause all sorts of problems, including scrambled files.)

When you have the Shuffle connected to the computer and see the amber light gently blinking on the front of the player, the computer sees it as an external drive and is not ready to let it go yet. Don't unplug the Shuffle when the amber light is blinking!

You have several ways to disconnect the Shuffle and keep the computer from complaining.

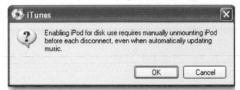

You can:

Click the Eject button in iTunes.

Click the Eject button next to the Shuffle's name in the iTunes Source list.

Click the Eject button in the Mac's Finder.

Click the Eject button next to the Shuffle's icon in the list of connected drives in the Mac OS X Finder window.

Click the Safely Remove Hardware feature in Windows.

Look in the Windows System Tray for the Safely Remove Hardware icon, which looks like a green arrow floating above a white square. Click the arrow icon, and then select the Shuffle from the list of attached devices to safely eject it from your computer.

Drag the Shuffle Icon to the Mac's Trash.

Clicking the Shuffle's desktop icon and then dragging it across the screen to the Trash will eject the drive, just like it does for CDs, DVDs, Zip disk, and other removable media.

Getting Started

iTunes

Filling Shuffle
with Music

Playing with
Playlists

Pocket USB
Drive

Cool Stuff for
iPod Shuffle

More Shuffle
Resources

Once the amber light stops blinking, it's safe to pull the Shuffle out of the USB port and move on with your life.

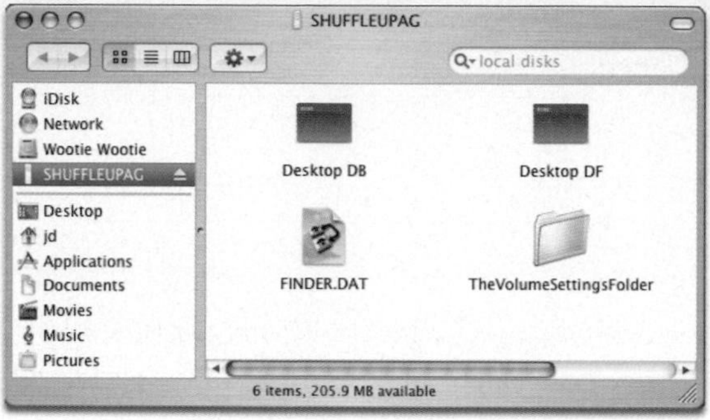

Cool Stuff for Your iPod Shuffle

Cool iPod Shuffle accessories

Your little green iPod Shuffle box has the bare essentials to get you up and rocking out with your new music player, but some people may need additional accessories to make the Shuffle work with their systems. Having USB ports that are too close together to fit the iPod Shuffle is one situation where accessory help might be needed.

Serious shoppers can find many of these Shuffle-specific accessories available on Apple's web site at *www.apple.com/ipodshuffle/accessories.html,* as well as in Apple Stores or other places that sell Apple products.

Cases

The iPod Shuffle comes with a white string neck lanyard, but wearing it this way may not work for runners or people working out who might get smacked in the face with their own Shuffles flying around. Luckily, there are other options for keeping your iPod Shuffle close at hand.

The iPod Shuffle Arm Band is one such carrying case that keeps the iPod Shuffle firmly strapped to your arm while you work out. It sells for about $30 and might be a good option for people who want their music within easy reach without having to wear it around their necks where it might get tangled up.

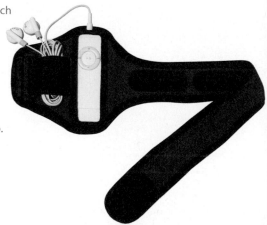

Nature-loving folks who exercise outdoors might like the *iPod Shuffle Sport Case,* which provides a protective cover to keep sand and water out of the Shuffle. It costs about $30 and comes with its own neck strap.

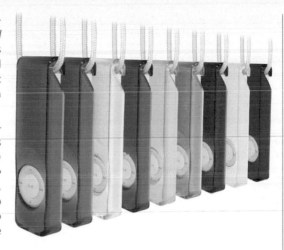

For about $17, you can get a *ShuffleMate* belt-clip holder that keeps your iPod Shuffle within easy reach. The ShuffleMate, available to order at *www.shufflemate.com,* also gives you a place to wind up your excess headphone cable so it's not flopping around loose and getting tangled up.

Sporting folks might like the $30 *XtremeMac SportWrap for iPod Shuffle.* This moisture-resistant armband comes in four colors gives you a slot for your Shuffle and a pocket to tuck away your headphones as well.

Griffin Technology, which makes scores of products for all kinds of iPods at *www.griffintechnology.com,* has produced a colorful metal case called the *iVault* for the iPod Shuffle. Available in silver, purple, red, or blue for about $30 from the company's web site, the iVault wraps your Shuffle in aluminum armor while still making the Shuffle ports easy to access.

Getting Started

iTunes

Filling Shuffle
with Music

Playing with
Playlists

Pocket USB
Drive

**Cool Stuff for
iPod Shuffle**

More Shuffle
Resources

iPod accessory stores on the Web

Many companies devote sections of their online stores to selling iPod-related merchandise, everything from cases to cables just for your iPod. Many of these companies are now stocking up on iPod Shuffle goodies.

The XtremeMac site (*www.xtrememac.com*) is a great place for one-stop shopping, no matter if you're in the market for a protective case for your Shuffle or the proper cables to connect it to your home stereo. The site also sells a car charger for juicing up your Shuffle's battery as you drive down the road and a Y-shaped adapter that allows two pairs of headphones to listen to the same iPod Shuffle.

EverythingiPod (*www.everythingipod.com*) has a 5-pack line of different lanyard end-caps to give your Shuffle a splash of color and also sells the $20 DLO Flip Clip that lets you snap your Shuffle right on your belt.

Other web shops that have nice cases for all kinds of iPods include The iStore (*www.theistore.com*) and Marware (*www.marware.com*).

Extra power for the iPod Shuffle

If your iPod Shuffle has problems because your USB ports don't have enough power or are too jammed together, you can get products to help you out. There's even a battery-life extender to give you more playtime on top of your regular 12-hour battery charge.

If your USB ports are hard to reach or are on the back of your computer, consider an *USB extension cable* that plugs into the port and snakes around to a more convenient place to plug in your Shuffle. You can usually find these cables for less than $10 at most computer stores. An extension cable can also come in handy if the Shuffle is too wide to fit in alongside the other devices plugged into your computer's ports.

If you want the same thing, only fancier, try *The iPod Shuffle Dock,* power-pedestal for your iPod Shuffle that costs about $30. It's a combination desktop stand and USB extension cord that lets your Shuffle sit up at attention while you have it hooked to the Mac or PC.

Getting Started

iTunes

Filling Shuffle
with Music

Playing with
Playlists

Pocket USB
Drive

**Cool Stuff for
iPod Shuffle**

More Shuffle
Resources

iPod
Shuffle
Fan Book

70

If you're going to be away from your computer or don't want to bother plugging in the Shuffle just to charge it, the *iPod USB Power Adapter* comes to the rescue. It looks like the AC adapter for an iBook or regular iPod, but you plug your Shuffle into the USB jack on one side and into the electrical outlet on the other and your Shuffle gets charged right from the wall. It sells for about $30.

If you want even more power, the *iPod Shuffle External Battery Pack* can get you up to 20 hours of playtime between charges, up from the normal 12 hours of tunes. This $30 attachment runs on two AA batteries that add a bit of weight to your iPod Shuffle, but you may not mind as long as there's music in your ears.

Headphones

Just about any pair of headphones with the 3.5-inch stereo miniplug will work with the iPod Shuffle, although some headphones are larger than the Shuffle itself. If you want to match your Shuffle, finding matching white headphones can be difficult, but more companies are making them these days.

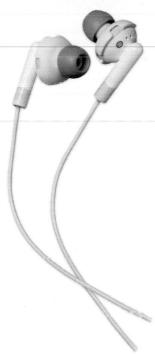

Philips Electronics makes the *HE592 Surround Sound Ear Buds* that you can find for around $25 in electronics stores or places like Amazon.com.

The Sony *MDR-J20 Vertical In-Ear Headphones* come in white and sell for around $20. The company makes plenty of headphones, including the $40 *Fontopia MDR-EX71SL/WK Ear Buds* that offer extra bass and come in white with silver and gray accents.

If you want to stick with the mother ship, try the nice, white *Apple In-Ear Headphones* that come with three different sizes of ear caps to make sure they fit inside a wide range of ears. The headphones can be found at *http://store.apple.com* and in Apple retail stores for about $40.

If you like the look of your iPod Shuffle's own headphones but wish they could pump out extra bass, check out Griffin Technology's EarJams for iPod at *www.griffintechnology.com*. These $15 attachments snap onto the end of the iPod ear buds to let them sit inside your ears a little farther while they boost your bass.

Getting Started

iTunes

Filling Shuffle
with Music

Playing with
Playlists

Pocket USB
Drive

**Cool Stuff for
iPod Shuffle**

More Shuffle
Resources

Car stereo helpers for the iPod Shuffle

Your tiny iPod Shuffle can take over your car's stereo, too, providing you have the right kind of equipment. For cars without a cassette player, try an FM transmitter like the $40 *Belkin Tune-Cast II* that plugs into the top of the Shuffle and beams its music out through an empty FM channel on the car's radio.

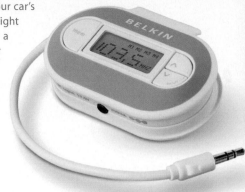

XtremeMac has an FM Transmitter designed just for the iPod Shuffle. The $50 *AirPlay for iPod Shuffle* snaps onto the end of the Shuffle and features an illuminated digital display so you can tell what frequency you're borrowing for your Shuffle tunes.

Most FM transmitters that plug into the Shuffle's headphone jack should work with your tiny iPod, although finding an empty FM frequency to borrow can be a challenge, especially if you live in a large urban area like New York, Chicago, or Los Angeles where there are already tons of radio stations hogging up all the available channels.

If you have a tape player in your car, you can get a special adapter that looks like a cassette with a wire coming out of one end. You plug the wire into the iPod Shuffle and the cassette part into the tape deck and the Shuffle's music comes out of the dashboard speakers. The *Sony CPA-9C Car Cassette Adapter* is available for about $20 at *http://store.apple.com* and a similar product, the *XtremeMac iPod Cassette Adapter* can be found for around $20 at *www.xtrememac.com*.

Cables to connect the iPod Shuffle to your home stereo

You can easily connect your iPod Shuffle to your home stereo and use your tiny iPod to fill the room with music through your system's speakers. All you need is a Y-shaped audio cable that has a 3.5-inch stereo miniplug on one end and a pair of red and white RCA plugs on the other end. Plug the miniplug into the Shuffle's headphones port and the RCA plugs into an available component jack on the back of your stereo system's audio receiver and you're ready to go.

Many companies make these Y-shaped cables. You can find one for as little as $7 at your local Radio Shack, or at places that specialize in audio-video wiring like MonsterCable*(www.monstercable.com)*. You can also use Griffin Technology's (*www.griffintechnology.com*) iPod Home Connection Kit (about $15) to connect any iPod to your stereo system.

iPod Shuffle shirts

Not long after the iPod Shuffle was announced, an enterprising company came up with a garment that literally lets you wear your iPod Shuffle on your sleeve. ShuffleShirt.com (*www.shuffleshirt.com*) has designed a series of t-shirts with sassy, Shuffle-centric slogans like "Sorry . . . I can't hear you. I'm shuffling." And "I shuffle . . . therefore I am." on the front and a handy Shuffle-sized pocket on the left sleeve. The shirts sell for about $20 and let you make both a musical statement *and* a fashion statement.

More iPod Shuffle Resources

7

Taking care of your iPod Shuffle now and later

Although it's a small and simple device to use, sometimes the iPod Shuffle can act funny or refuse to play nice. Damaged hardware is sometimes a possibility, but often the problem is just a miscommunication between hardware and software or even something minor that can be healed with a quick fix. Here are some of the minor problems you may encounter with your Shuffle and what to do about them.

This chapter also tells you where to find more information about the iPod Shuffle and where iPod fanatics like to hang out on the Web so you can drop by and find out all the latest iPod Shuffle news.

How to reset your iPod Shuffle

If you Shuffle is acting weird and refusing to play music or skipping around, sometimes a good swift hardware reset will take care of things. This is just like rebooting your computer, except it's easier.

1. Disconnect the iPod Shuffle if you have it plugged into your computer.
2. Flip the Shuffle over and slide the switch on the back to the Off position so that the green stripe is hidden.
3. Wait about 5 seconds.
4. Slide the switch on the back to Shuffle or to the Play In Order setting.

Your iPod Shuffle is now reset.

Updating and restoring the iPod shuffle's software

If your computer won't recognize the iPod Shuffle no matter what you do, odds are the Shuffle's operating system may be messed up and need to be reinstalled. (This can sometimes happen if you unplug the Shuffle when the amber light is blinking.)

You may have already installed the iPod Updater program on your computer when you installed the software on the iPod CD when you first got your Shuffle. If it's been awhile since you bought your iPod Shuffle, you can get a copy of the latest iPod Shuffle software online at *www.apple.com/ipod/download*.

If Apple has released an update for the iPod software and your computer is set to check for iTunes and iPods updates automatically in iTunes→Preferences→General (Mac) or Edit→Preferences→General (Windows), you may get a message on your screen asking if you want to update your software.

iTunes has detected a software update for the iPod "SHUFFLEUPAG". Would you like to install it now?

Cancel   OK

Getting Started

iTunes

Filling Shuffle
with Music

Playing with
Playlists

Pocket USB
Drive

Cool Stuff for
iPod Shuffle

More Shuffle
Resources

When you first start the iPod Updater program, you are presented with two choices: Update or Restore. As with the big hard drive–based iPods, *Update* just puts a replacement or newer version of the system software on the Shuffle and leaves your songs and data undisturbed, while *Restore* wipes everything completely off the drive and makes you reload all of your songs and files from the computer.

① Once you've downloaded the iPod Updater file to your computer, double-click the installer file and follow the onscreen instructions.

② Connect the iPod Shuffle to the computer.

③ Most Macs will start the update right away, but if your Windows PC doesn't know what to do, point it to Start→All Programs→iPod and choose the updater file with the most recent date.

④ Click Update or Restore and let the software guide you through the process.

If the iPod software updater doesn't realize you have your player plugged in already, flip the Shuffle off and then back on again.

After you have restored or updated your iPod Shuffle, take it for a spin and see if it behaves better. If you still have problems with it, there may be something wrong with its internal hardware that might mean a visit to the Frequently Asked Questions page for iPod Shuffle service at *www.apple.com/support/ipodshuffle/service/faq* to see possible repair options.

The iPod Shuffle Support page is another good place to visit and has plenty of information, user guides, tutorials, and links to other important Shuffle matters at *www.apple.com/support/ipodshuffle*.

If you have the wrong version of Windows . . .

If someone has given you an iPod Shuffle for a gift and your PC is too old to work with iTunes, you might have another option for getting the player to work with Windows 98 or Windows Me.

At least two companies make programs designed to let iPods talk to older versions of Windows. Check out XPlay (*www.mediafour.com*) or Anapod Explorer (*www.redchairsoftware.com*) if you're in the market for a program you can use instead of iTunes for moving songs to your Shuffle. Each sells for around $30, but you can download a sample version to try before you buy.

Getting Started

iTunes

Filling Shuffle
with Music

Playing with
Playlists

Pocket USB
Drive

Cool Stuff for
iPod Shuffle

More Shuffle
Resources

The iPod Shuffle's buttons don't respond

Unlike regular iPods, the iPod Shuffle doesn't have a Hold switch to temporarily disable the controls to prevent an accidental button push by bump. To put a Shuffle on Hold, you have to press down on the Play/Pause button for a few seconds until the amber light flashes to indicate that it's locked up. Sometimes this can happen without your realizing it.

If you find your Shuffle's buttons aren't responding, try pressing the Play/Pause button for another few seconds. If the green light on the front flashes three times, the Shuffle was on hold and you've just released it.

If that doesn't work, there are a few other things to consider trying, such as resetting the iPod Shuffle.

It's also possible that your Shuffle's battery has run out of power. If the battery status light on the back shows a red light—or no light at all—when you press it, try charging up the Shuffle for a few hours to see if its buttons return to normal.

If none of the suggestions above work, try restoring the Shuffle's software.

iPod
Shuffle
Fan Book

The iPod Shuffle pages at Apple.com

Apple's web site has many areas devoted to all things iPod, including iTunes, the iTunes Music Store, and cool things to buy for your iPod Shuffle.

The iPod Shuffle home page

All the basic information about the iPod Shuffle is here, along with short video demonstrations, technical specifications, and a link to the feedback area so you can tell Apple how you really feel about your iPod Shuffle (*www.apple.com/ipodshuffle*).

Apple Service & Support

This is the starter page for finding support on any Apple hardware or software product, and it also lists the most recent versions of its popular programs (like iTunes) in case you're feeling slightly out of date (*www.apple.com/ support*).

The iPod Shuffle Support page

The iPod Shuffle support page (*www.apple.com/support/ipodshuffle*) highlights many of the most popular Shuffle troubleshooting articles in Apple's great big Knowledge Base of technical fix-it articles for the iPod Shuffle.

Taking care of your iPod now and later

7

Getting Started

iTunes

Filling Shuffle
with Music

Playing with
Playlists

Pocket USB
Drive

Cool Stuff for
iPod Shuffle

More Shuffle
Resources

iTunes Support for Mac OS X

Apple keeps a collection of top iTunes support articles and tutorials for Mac mavens all in one convenient place (*www.apple.com/support/itunes*).

ITunes Support for Windows

PC people can find answers to technical questions or issues unique to the Windows version of iTunes, plus topic-based tutorials on how to use iTunes (*www.apple.com/support/itunes/windows*).

Technical Discussions

Apple's forums give both veterans and newbies a place to discuss support issues and directly ask technical questions about issues they may be having with the iPod Shuffle and iTunes on both Mac OS X and Windows. Go here if you haven't been able to find the answer in the Knowledge Base (*http://discussions.info.apple.com*).

The Apple Store

You can buy an iPod Shuffle, iPod Shuffle accessories, and oodles of other Apple hardware and software right from the source (*http://store.apple.com*).

Other fun iPod web sites

Apple has plenty of pages devoted to its products, but if you want a more unorthodox view, you can't beat the crazy, cranky, brilliant commentary found on many of the devoted iPod fan web sites.

iPodHacks

iPodHacks (*www.ipodhacks.com*) boasts a lively forum and plenty of tech talk, in addition to updates from around the Podsphere.

iPoding

The iPoding site (*www.ipoding.com*) is another good stop for iPod news and has been spreading Pod Knowledge since the early days of the 5-gigabyte Mac-only original iPod.

iPodLounge

iPodLounge (*www.ipodlounge.com*) is one of the most comprehensive iPod-related sites on the Web. It's crammed with breaking news, user reviews, technical tips, and plenty of fun, and covers every model of iPod ever produced. The site has its own Tips & Tricks section, a Frequently Asked Questions list, and lots of opinions on its message boards.

Index